BARBARIANS

Text by Tim Newark
Colour plates by Angus McBride
B/W illustrations by Edward Haney

D1133341

Copyright © 1998
by CONCORD PUBLICATIONS CO.
603-609 Castle Peak Road
Kong Nam Industrial Building
10/F, B1, Tsuen Wan
New Territories, Hong Kong

All rights reserved. No part of
this publication may be reproduced,
stored in a retrieval system or
transmitted in any form or by any
means, electronic, mechanical,
photocopying or otherwise, without
the prior written permission of
Concord Publications Co.

We welcome authors who can help
expand our range of books. If you
would like to submit material,
please feel free to contact us.

We are always on the look-out for new,
unpublished photos for this series.
If you have photos or slides or
information you feel may be useful to
future volumes, please send them to us
for possible future publication.
Full photo credits will be given upon
publication.
ISBN962-361-634-1
printed in Hong Kong

*Concord Publications would like to acknowledge the
assistance of Ken Mosbaugh in this project.*

Introduction

In 1930, a German politician visited the archaeological museum in Nuremberg. 'What enormous migrations those must have been,' he enthused, 'carried out over centuries and millennia by those inhabitants of northern Europe and Asia. What battles must have taken place as tribes decided to spread out toward the south... Such times also generally breed great leaders among peoples.' In 1933, the same politician was more open about his inspiration gained from these ancient peoples. 'Yes, we are barbarians!' he declared. 'We want to be barbarians! It is an honourable title. We shall rejuvenate the world! This world is near its end. It is our mission to cause unrest.' The politician was now Chancellor of the German nation and his name was Adolf Hitler.

When the Panzers rolled into France and Italy, the code-names Hitler chose for these campaigns were Attila and Alaric, both mighty barbarian warlords, and he sought to outdo them in both conquest and brutality. In this Hitler succeeded, adding his own name to that long list of barbarian warlords that have terrorised civilisation. That Hitler chose to identify himself with the violence and destruction of these barbarian peoples is in direct opposition to our late 20th century sensibilities in which historians seek to show how these ancient tribesmen were actually quite sophisticated people adept at trade and other peaceful activities. These two opposing views of the barbarians say as much about our own times as they do of the tribesmen who lived two thousand years ago. Today, the West wishes to be viewed as a tolerant culture in which stereotypes are revealed as bogus. Seventy years ago, the West believed it had become too civilised, was decadent in its own prosperity and comfort, and deserved a war led by energetic new forces. Hitler was one of only many people at that time that believed in the refreshing nature of barbarian invasions.

With these two widely differing interpretations lodged in our minds, it is thus very difficult to view the Germanic and Asian barbarians with any objectivity. Indeed, any attempt at trying to see them through their own eyes is almost impossible as they left barely any written evidence of their own lives. In the 1st or the 5th centuries AD, we invariably see them through the eyes of Greeks or Romans. To begin with, they viewed these alien tribesmen as strangers speaking incomprehensible languages, but as the tribesmen grew more confident and demanded more from the Mediterranean, Latin and Greek scholars demonised them as destroyers of civilisation and this is largely the view [...] popular imagination.

In reality, though the barbarians certainly overturned the ancient political state of Rome, they nevertheless maintained much of Roman and Greek culture and if they failed to reach any new heights of civilisation in the so-called Dark Ages, it was more out of incompetence rather than malice. The Modernist belief fashionable at the beginning of this century that Dark Ages Christian culture was simply different, and not inferior to, Classical Pagan culture, might again say more about the desire of Modernist artists, than about a reality that does seem to point at a loss of skills from the 4th century onwards in such endeavours as art and science. But such an investigation might well point at uncomfortable truths in our own post-literate society in which images triumph over the written word and formal education is swamped by non-judgemental philosophies. Such is the continuing impact of the barbarians and their assault on the ancient order.

This book is essentially a military review of the barbarian invasions from the 5th century BC to the 10th century AD in Europe. In it we see successive waves of barbarian peoples from the Celts and the Scythians to the Vikings and Magyars. All these were considered barbaric by their victims who also understood the way they fought as something different from their own organised and more formal attitudes to battle. The barbarian was a hit-and-run warrior. He was not paid to fight, but lived off his loot. Thus, raiding against soft targets suited his sense of survival much more than a clash of hoplites or legionaries. Whenever possible, he avoided a set battle. Horse riding suited this mode of warfare best and from the Celts in the West to the Huns in the East, the majority of barbarians were excellent horse warriors.

The main difference within barbarian warfare was that Western warriors such as the Celts and Germans preferred to use spears and swords in close combat, whereas the Huns and other Turkic warriors preferred to fight at a distance with bow and arrow. That said, such was the interconnection between these two main fighting cultures that barbarian armies invariably incorporated both styles side by side, the Ostrogoths, or Eastern Goths, being a classic example, combining both steppe warrior harassment and a Germanic aristocratic desire for hand-to-hand combat.

(Plate 1)

Were the Celts the very first barbarians? The word 'barbarian' originated as a Greek term describing any foreigner. It was in imitation of their babbling incomprehensible speech, but it could equally apply to a Scythian or a Persian as well as a Celt. It was not then a derogatory term, describing someone who is uncivilised or savage. That came later and derived from the Latin association of barbari with the Germanic and Eurasian tribes that eventually brought down the Roman Empire.

To the ancient Greeks, the Celts were not necessarily any less civilised or cultured than they were. Indeed, Greek philosophy is said to be in part derived from the wisdom of Celtic sages. They were, however, regarded as an especially fierce race of warriors and as such were both feared as raiders and respected as mercenaries. The Romans had a similarly ambivalent attitude to the Celts. They feared them as fighters, but they also gained much from their culture, including the use of armour, both mail and various forms of helmets copied directly from the Celts. In later centuries, the Celts would settle most easily into the world of the Roman Empire, adopting its culture and styles for their own and helping the Romans fight against the Germanic barbarians. But despite this equality of culture and mutual respect, there were two great incidents which were barbaric in nature—in the later, brutal sense of the word—which do present the Celts as the original barbarians from the north. The first was the sack and destruction of Delphi in Greece, the holiest of ancient Greek religious sites, in the 3rd century BC (this has been described in the previous title Ancient Celts). The second came earlier in 390 BC when Rome was attacked and its people humiliated.

The Celtic assault on Rome, foreshadowing events almost a thousand years later, began with their entry into northern Italy. For years previously they had extended their grip on this land, fighting the Etruscans as they went. In 391 BC, the Etruscans called on the Romans for help and the Romans warned the Celts to go no further. The Celts, under the leadership of a chieftain called Brennos (derived from a Celtic word meaning 'king' and possibly not referring to an individual but a title, as it was another Brennos who sacked Delphi), took this as a challenge. The next year, the Celts arrived in force and clashed with a Roman army on the banks of the Allia, barely ten miles from their capital. The Celts attacked in their usual style, a bellowing charge with swords and spears. Panic spread through the Roman ranks 'at the first sound of the Celtic war cry on their flank and in their rear,' records Livy. The Roman soldiers 'hardly

waited even to see their strange enemy from the ends of the earth.. None fell fighting, cut down from behind as they struggled to force a way to safety through the heaving mass of their fellow fugitives.' It was a classic Celtic victory, obtained in that first furious onslaught The road to Rome was now wide open.

The citizens of Rome retreated to the core of their city around the Capitol and the Celts laid siege to it for seven months Eventually, the Romans decided to buy their way out of trouble and presented an enormous ransom to Brennos. When the Romans complained at the weights used to measure their gold, Brennos threw his iron sword on to the balance and declared 'woe to the conquered'. It was a brutal truth the Romans would never forget or forgive and this legend underpinned much of the ferocity of their later conquest of Celtic lands. The Celts depicted in the painting are of this period, described as La Tene culture in their history. They are clad in bronze armour and are armed with iron swords and spears. They are leaving a lake-side dwelling typical of those inhabited along the banks of lakes in Central Europe, the homeland of the Celts before they invaded northern Italy.

4

Scythian raiders in Thrace, 5th century BC

(Plate 2)

The Scythians were the first great tribe of warrior horsemen from the steppes to make an impact on the Western imagination. So much so that they became a generic term for nomadic horsemen from the lands north and east of the Black Sea and the name of their country, Scythia, appeared on maps long after their culture had been swept away by other confederations of steppe warriors. Their clothing of zig-zag patterned trousers and hoods and their archetypal weapon the bow made them an instantly recognisable type of barbarian appearing on countless Greek vases and scepters. Later Roman writers, perhaps hoping to give their histories some of the authority of those written by the ancient Greeks, even called the Huns by the name Scyth and this would have been clearly understood by their readers. Arrian, writing in the second century AD, describes their classic tactics in a confrontation with Alexander the Great: "They made circles around the small attacking force, shooting as they rode, and then galloped off to a safe distance." This method of "safe" warfare in which the Scythians harrassed weaker formations with showers of arrow was in stark contrast to the method of contact warfare devised by the Greeks, in which formations clashed in hand-to-hand fighting, and served to make them the classic barbarians of the steppes with every other later horse-borne raider fighting in the same style.

Archaeological and literary evidence places the Scythians north of the Black Sea in southern Russia in the land now known as the Ukraine. Unlike later waves of steppe nomads, they did not speak a Turkic language and were not related to Turkic or Mongol groups. They were Indo-European in appearance and spoke an Iranian tongue which brought them more closely to the Medes and Persians. Herodotus is the first great Greek chronicler of the Scythians in the 5th century BC and it is from him that we have some of the classic images of steppe life, such as when a great Scythian leader was buried his horses were killed and stuffed, being supported on poles around his tomb, or the skulls of their enemies being used as drinking goblets. His greatest military account is to tell the story of Darius, the Persian emperor, and his attempt to invade Scythia.

Around 512 BC, Darius crossed into Europe from the Persian empire, his intention being to conquer Greece. Before he could do this, he needed to secure Thrace from the raids of the Scythians. Using a pontoon bridge to cross the Danube, he entered Scythian territory. The Persian army was of considerable size and the Scythian leadership employed the classic strategy of the Russian steppes. Retreating before it, they burned grass, poisoned wells, and drove off cattle. One half of the Scythian force drew the army on, deeper into their territory, while the other half shadowed it, preventing it from turning away to more vulnerable land. After several weeks of this the Persian emperor grew tired and sent a messenger to the Scythian King.

"Strange man," asked Darius, "why do you always run away? You could choose to stand and fight if you consider yourself strong enough. But if you believe you are weak, then why not stop this running and make your submission to me, bringing me gifts of land and water?"

"I have never fled for fear of any man," replied the king of the Scythians. "I do not flee from you now, but travel as I always do in peace. But if you wish to know why we do not fight you, it is because we do not possess towns or farmlands that would force us to protect them. But if you do wish to battle with us, then seek our fathers' tombs for then you will find out whether we fight or not. Until then we shall not battle you."

Instead of gifts, the Scythians sent parties of horse-archers to harass the Persians while they searched for food. Finally, Darius gave up and turned his army back towards the Danube. It was then the Scythians struck in force. Their horse-archers galloped forward, followed by more heavily armoured Scythian nobles. Darius hurriedly ordered his warriors into their formations and awaited battle, but as the two armies faced each other, a hare popped up and bounded across the plain. The Scythians liked nothing better than to hunt. Despite being prepared for battle, they could not resist the tiny creature and a body of horsemen broke away from the Scythian army, chasing it wildly with whoops of excitement. Darius asked his adviser for an explanation and was greatly depressed by the answer. "Do the Scythians regard us with such contempt?" he sighed. "They have had nothing but sport with us." Without waiting any further opportunity of battle, Darius ordered his men home. The Scythians had won and the steppes would remain free from the conquest of any western empire, even the Romans.

The painting shows a heavily armed party of Scythian raiders in Thrace. They wear scale armour, typical of their culture and later worn by Sarmatians as depicted by the Romans. They carry bows, spears, swords, and an axe called a sagaris. Their equipment is elaborate and expensive, putting a lie to the belief that nomads are poor—raiders such as this could draw not only on their own wealth derived from their extensive herds of livestock, but also that extracted from the Greeks.

(Plate 3)

Pliny the Elder describes the appeal of Italy for the Celts in a surprisingly contemporary and trivial manner, much more in tune with our own consumer world. "The Celts, imprisoned as they were by the Alps," he says, "first found a motive for entering into Italy from a Celt of the Helvetti named Helico who lived in Rome as a craftsman and brought back with him some dried figs and grapes and samples of oil and wine. It is no surprise then they should seek to obtain these things by war!" Plutarch, taking a similar tone, ascribes their advance into Italy to their love of wine, not the first time that alcohol would be seen to play a special role in the affairs of the Celts.

Although it would be the Romans who would eventually feel the power of the Celts, it was the Etruscans who suffered most from their early incursions and, indeed, may well have been fatally weakened by them in their own competition with Rome, allowing the Romans to ultimately overtake their own lands. Starting in the 5th century, the Celtic invasion of northern Italy grew more intense by the beginning of the 4th century. Sites near present-day Milan and Bologna became principal Celtic settlements. Further south, they contested Etruscan land, fought great battles, and burial sites featuring La Tene iron swords have been found. The Romans now referred to northern Italy as Cisalpine Gaul.

Seeing themselves sandwiched between the growing powers of the Celts and the Romans, the Etruscans decided to form an alliance with the Celts and paid the tribesmen money to march on Rome, but at the last moment the Celts pulled out, claiming the Etruscans had paid them protection money, not for fighting against the Romans, although they were willing to consider this in turn for grants of Etruscan land. Polybius records another occasion when the Celts did join with the Etruscans in a raid on Roman territory, "but no sooner had they arrived home than they began to argue about obtaining a larger share of the spoils and in the end destroyed the greater part of their own army and even the loot itself."

By the 3rd century BC, not even the alliance of Etruscan and Celt could stop the expansion of the Roman state and several joint armies were annihilated by a now resurgent Roman army used to dealing with Celtic warriors. Dionysius describes how the new Roman short stabbing sword could be used more effectively against the long iron slashing swords of the Celts: "agile their foes were, still raising their swords aloft, but the Romans would duck under their arms, holding up their shields, and then stooping and crouching low, they would render vain and useless the blows of others, which were aimed too high, while waiting for their own part, holding their swords straight out, they would strike their opponents in the groin, pierce their sides, and drive their blows through their breasts into their vitals." With armour and long body shields adopted from the Celts, the Romans had reached a military maturity, gained from these battles with Etruscans and Celts that would allow them to rapidly conquer the rest of the Mediterranean.

The painting depicts a war band of Celts in northern Italy in the first half of the 4th century BC. They are about to descend on an Etruscan settlement. Their arms and armour is typical of the La Tene culture. The chief warrior's helmet is adorned with wings, a favourite Celtic motif. "On their heads they wear bronze helmets," records Diodorus Siculus, "which possess large projecting figures of enormous stature to the wearer. In some cases horns form one part with the helmet, while in other cases it is relief figures of the fore parts of birds or animals." The horned helmet, so beloved of early representations of Vikings, is thus presented as a Celtic invention. Diodorus also describes their characteristic shields: "for arms they have man-sized shields decorated in a manner peculiar to them. Some of these have projecting figures in bronze, skilfully wrought not only for decoration but for protection."

(Plate 4)

Alexander the Great considered himself a god. When he chose to immortalise his image on coins, he was portrayed with horns, the sign of the god Dionysus. Dionysus was the wild god, the god of the impetuous, violent spirit that lurks inside men and women and is liberated by alcohol. A son of Zeus, Dionysus left his homeland to roam across the world accompanied by a licentious army of satyrs and maenads, spreading the use of wine, conquering armies in Egypt and Asia, and marching as far afield as India. Here was a model for Alexander's ambition and a sign that the way he lived could lead to remarkable conquests. Even his passion for alcohol was central to this, the chroniclers telling of his wild drinking sessions in which even his friends sometimes fell victim to his violence. A man such as this was not likely to expect anything other than complete submission from barbarian tribesmen—but then Alexander had never met Celtic warriors before.

Alexander's campaign to the land of the Celts occurred early in his military career and was a prelude to his conquest of Asia. It was very much an operation to secure the northern borders of his homeland of Macedonia from the tribes that raided across the Danube river, the traditional dividing line between the civilised south and the barbarian north. At first, he subdued the Thracians, Illyrians, and Triballians, and then he closed on the Danube. Battle ships awaited him, having been sent up river from Byzantium, but these proved ineffective in dealing with the swift currents and steep banks of the river and so he resorted to gathering simple dug-out boats, used by the locals for fishing, and thus ferried his army across. The crossing took place at night, but on the other side awaiting him was an army of the Getae. Variously described as Dacian, Germanic, or Celtic tribesmen, the Getae were probably a mixture of all three cultures. Perhaps surprised by the speed of the crossing, the Getae proved a poor foe for Alexander who used both cavalry and the Macedonian phalanx to clear them out of the way. He then looted their town and burnt it to the ground. Alexander had proved his domination of the area and now awaited the submission of other tribes from further afield.

Among the barbarian envoys that visited Alexander's encampment on the Danube was a group of Celts—"men of haughty demeanour and tall in proportion" is how Arrian describes them, our principal source for this encounter. Sensibly the Celts were there to offer their friendship to the Macedonian warlord and mutual vows of peace were made, but Alexander just had to push it a little further. Flush with his recent victories, he asked the Celts what they

were afraid of most in the world, expecting them to submit further and declare "You, my lord." But the Celts were a practical and straight-talking race, taking the subject of their fears very seriously. "We fear only that the sky fall and crush us," they announced, "or the earth open and swallow us, or the sea rise and overwhelm us." Alexander was furious, but he let the slight go, remarking instead under his breath that the Celts thought too much of themselves. A peace was made, but the Celts had simply bought themselves time. Some fifty years later, the Celts would ride into Macedonia and Greece and devastate the very heartland of Alexander's empire.

The success of the Celtic raiding campaign of 279 BC is all the more remarkable when one bears in mind that just a few decades earlier, the Greek war machine had subdued much of Asia. The difference, of course, was Alexander and with his achievements in disarray following his death and a group of successor warlords fighting for control, the Greek city states were especially vulnerable. Having killed the king of Macedonia, the Celtic raiding force under Brennos made for Thermopylae and defeated an Athenian led force. The prosperous lands of Greece were now exposed and the Celts headed for one of its richest sites—the sacred temple of Delphi, loaded with rich dedications to the gods. In a mighty storm, with thunder and lightning crashing about them, the Celts breached the defences of Delphi and sacked its treasures. It was an insult to the gods that had, perhaps, been foreshadowed by the Celtic act of defiance to the living god Alexander those fifty years beforehand.

Celtiberian warriors with Roman prisoner, late 2nd century BC

(Plate 5)

In an age that was no stranger to ruthless violence, even contemporaries considered the war in Spain in the 2nd century BC to be particularly brutal. "This war between the Romans and Celtiberians is called the fiery war," wrote Polybius, "for while wars in Greece or Asia are settled with one or two pitched battles, the battles there dragged on, only brought to a temporary end by the darkness of night. Both sides refused to let their courage flag or their bodies tire." For Republican Rome, it was their Vietnam, a vicious guerrilla war creating a spiral of atrocities that served only to entrench both sides further, causing even Roman politicians to question way they were there in the first place. The Celtiberians were descendants of Celtic invaders who had entered Spain some centuries earlier when the Celts were moving from their central European homeland westwards. They retained the Celtic talent for warfare, being ferocious warriors who would never ever let a grudge rest, preferring instead to impoverish their country rather than give in to an outsider. In the Romans they met an enemy who was just as determined to fight to the bitter end, whatever the cost.

A typical incident in the war was perpetrated by Titus Didius who invited one group of Celtiberians to fight with him and thus acquire the land of a neighbouring tribe. He invited the warriors to his encampment to discuss the terms of the alliance, but first they had to leave their weapons at the entrance to the stockade. Once inside, Didius had the gates locked and sent in his own troops to massacre every man, woman and child inside. "For this," remarked the disgusted Roman chronicler Appian; "Didius was actually honoured with a triumph." The Celtiberians returned the blow with atrocities of their own, causing even Scipio Africanus, that great veteran of the wars against Carthage, to despair: "They are no better than bandits. They may be brave when devastating neighbouring fields, burning villages, and rustling cattle, but are worth nothing in a regular army. They fight with greater confidence in flight than in their weapons." Such is a description of great guerrilla fighters. After half a century of this warfare, it took Publius Cornelius Scipio, grandson of Scipio Africanus, to bring some discipline to the struggle.

Scipio arrived in Spain in 134 BC to find a thoroughly demoralised Roman Army reduced to employing astrologers for any sign of future victory. Immediately, he expelled any hangers-on from the camp and sought to bring a sense of method and purpose to his troops. His first major challenge was the hillfort of Numantia. It was a massive fortification defended by ravines on two sides and wood and stone stockades. Scipio set about its defeat in such a methodical and precise manner that he may well have inspired Julius Caesar who used similar means against the hillfort of Alesia a century later. At first, Scipio denuded the surrounding area of any useful supplies, stockpiling them for his men and then burning the rest. He then proceeded to encircle Numantia with fortifications of his own, creating a great ring of seven forts linked by palisades and ditches. When this ring was completed, he then built another one to defend himself from any relieving forces. To prevent the Numantines receiving supplies from the rivers that ran through the ravines, Scipio erected towers on either side from which he hung heavy logs studded with spikes on a rope that stopped any boats passing by. Despite many assaults on the surrounding siegeworks, the Numantiens could found no way out and eventually starvation did its work. With characteristic Roman thoroughness, Scipio had the majority of them sold into slavery, burnt the town to the ground, and divided the land among their neighbours, thus bringing to an end one of the most brutal of wars.

The painting shows two Celtiberian warriors about to cut the head off a captured Roman soldier. The Celtiberians are armed with their characteristic falcata, great meat cleavers that were feared among the Romans. According to Livy, these cutlass blades could "cut off arms at the shoulder and sever heads with one chop." Archaeological remnants show Celtiberian warriors wearing Greek-style crested helmets.

Celt fighting German, Central Europe, c.100 BC

(Plate 6)

There was no love lost between the Celts and the Germans. Speaking different languages and from different racial roots, they were rivals for the lands and incomes of central and northern Europe for hundreds of years. They fought each other as warrior bands in endless feuds and they fought each other as part of large confederations in frontier wars. They raided and looted each other and they sold each other into slavery.

Even before the Romans imposed a frontier between the Romanised Celts inside the Empire and the barbarian Germans outside the Empire, there was a major cultural fault line between the two peoples that followed roughly the flow of the Rhine and Danube rivers. The Celts in their hillforts surrounded by farming land and settled communities may well have even considered the less highly developed Germans as barbarians. Certainly the wealth of Gallic France appears to have attracted the Germans across the Rhine in raids on these more prosperous lands, whereas there was no great pull for the Celts in the other direction, apart from sending out merchants to trade in furs and amber with the northern tribes.

Julius Caesar made great capital out of the hatred between the Germans and the Celts during his invasion of France in the 1st century BC. Previously, the Gallic tribes had employed German warriors in their own internecine warfare, but now the Germans were exploiting this situation and the Gauls called upon Caesar and the Romans to protect them from the Germans. "There was a time when the Gauls were more warlike than the Germans," wrote Caesar, "when they actually invaded German territory... (but) gradually accustomed to inferiority and defeated in many battles, they (the Celts) do not even pretend to compete with the Germans in bravery." Caesar paints a picture of Gauls softened by their access to Mediterranean civilisation, whereas the Germans remained poor and hardy, hungry for military success. Caesar respected only the Belgae who had been hardened by decades of border fighting with the Germans in northern France and may well have had mingled German and Celtic blood.

Throughout his campaigns in Gaul, Caesar frequently called upon German warriors to assist him against their traditional enemies. This was especially so at the siege of Alesia when many of his Celtic auxiliaries had deserted him to throw in their lot with Vercingetorix in a last stand against Roman conquest. In this final conflict in 52 BC, German horse warriors battled against Celts and gained for Caesar the decisive victory that broke Celtic power in France. From then on, the Celts would be the allies of the Romans and the German barbarians would be their joint enemy until the fall of Rome itself.

The painting depicts a clash between a Celt and a German around 100 BC and evokes the relative difference in culture and prosperity between the two peoples. The German warrior is bare-chested and wears animal furs with some jewellery perhaps captured from his Celtic adversaries. "They spend all their lives in hunting and warlike pursuits," wrote Caesar, "and inure themselves from childhood to toil and hardship... The Germans are not farmers and live principally on milk, cheese and meat." He goes on to describe how they hunt giant wild bulls called aurochs whose horns they cut off and mount with silver as ceremonial drinking cups. This wild natural style was exactly what the Romans considered barbaric.

In contrast, the Celtic warrior looks almost Mediterranean with his bronze breastplate, iron crested helmet and coloured tunic, revealing the cross-cultural influences that ran back and forth between the Celts and the Greek and Roman worlds. It is no surprise that the Celts should, on the whole, fit most comfortably into the Roman Empire and exploit it to their own ends. The heads of victims attached to his bronze boar standard, however, provides a reminder of their fierce warrior tradition. The German pits his cheaper, smaller weapons of axe, dagger, and spear against the luxurious iron sword of the Celt.

(Plate 7)

Britain was the final Celtic bastion to fall to the Roman conquerors. Britain now joined Northern Italy, France, and Spain, all Celtic realms, within the Empire. An expeditionary campaign by Caesar was followed by a more thorough invasion by the Emperor Claudius in 43 AD. Just as with Gaul, it was the internecine struggles between the Celtic tribes that proved the excuse for Roman intervention and the Romans continued to dominate Britain partly by understanding this and incorporating friendly tribal heads as their allies. But occupation was far from an easy ride. It is true that many Celtic warlords welcomed the peace and prosperity brought by the Romans, but others resented it profoundly and two revolts shook the pretensions of the Roman governors. Queen Boudicca's revolt in the south of England is the best known of these and the most violent, but equally threatening was that of Caratacus.

In 51 AD, retreating before the Roman advance, Caratacus drew his line of confrontation in Wales with the support of the Silures tribe. A land of mountains and marshes, Wales is a perfect land for guerrilla warfare, but Caratacus chose to centre his forces on a hillfort, a great error as the Romans had perfected their assaults on such fortresses and marched towards it under cover of a shield wall while their engineers dug away at the earth ramparts. The hillfort collapsed and the Romans slaughtered the Celts, Caratacus just managing to escape. He fled northwards to the land of another warrior Queen called Cartimandua. Caratacus, however, had misjudged any sense of Celtic brotherhood, for Cartimandua immediately had the Celtic king chained and handed over to the Romans, thus securing her own rule in the north of England as a client chieftain of the Romans.

The Britons fought much as the Celts of France did, with one major exception. They appear to have retained the use of the chariot long after it disappears in continental warfare. Caesar was especially impressed by their use in battle: "The chariots of the Britons begin the fighting by charging over the battlefield. From them they hurl javelins, although the noise of the wheels and chariot teams are enough to throw any enemy into panic. The charioteers are very skilled. They can drive their teams down very steep slopes without losing control. Some warriors can run along the chariot pole, stand on the yoke and then dart back into the chariot." Roman historian Tacitus describes a battle against northern Britons in which the Britons seem to be at a disadvantage against the German auxiliaries employed by the Romans. "The fighting began with

exchanges of missiles," he wrote, "the Britons showing both steadiness and skill in parrying our javelins with their huge swords or catching them on their little shields, while they themselves rained volleys on us." But when the Britons clash with the German auxiliaries, it is a different story. "These old soldiers (the Germans) had been well drilled in sword-fighting, while the enemy were awkward at it, with their small shields and unwieldy swords, especially as the later had no points and were quite unsuitable for cut and thrust at close quarters."

Beyond the Celts of northern England lived another kind of barbarian people—the Picts. These are generally regarded as non-Celtic tribesmen, perhaps related to the original inhabitants of Britain who were themselves displaced by invading waves of Celts. There is little evidence of this, however, and they may well just have been a northern confederation of Celtic tribesmen otherwise known as the Caledonii. From the evidence of other countries invaded by superior cultures, it is more than likely that the conquering Celts annihilated all the indigenous peoples, hunting them down as Westerners did in North America or Australia. The Picts' Latin name was inspired by the practice of covering their bodies in tattoos and they do appear to have devised a form of warfare different to that south of Hadrian's Wall. In this, long spears were used in a form of phalanx incorporating other warriors armed with swords and shields. The use of long spears or pikes is distinct to this part of Britain and appears later in Scottish warfare in the Middle Ages where a pike formation is known as the schiltron.

Alamanni break into a Roman fort, German border, 3rd century AD

(Plate 8)

The 3rd century was a testing time for the Roman Empire. The German tribes to the north of the Rhine and Danube were no longer the impoverished raiders of the 1st century, content with occasional forays into the prosperous south, mere pinpricks against the might of Roman civilisation. Through closer association with the Celts and Romans of the great border towns, these Germans had grown in sophistication and realised their potential for more significant gains.

Many of the brightest and most dynamic of these German warriors served with the Roman army, some even rising within its ranks to enjoy the luxury of the Roman elite. When they returned to their homelands, they brought with them new ambitions and this realised itself in the form of new alignments among the German peoples. The older, smaller tribes known by Caesar and Tacitus disintegrated and were replaced by large confederations headed by warlords selected not for their status within an individual tribe, but for their ability to lead a major army into battle. In central Europe, the most important of these new confederations was the Alammani—a Germanic name meaning "all people".

The first serious incursion of the Alamanni occurred in 213 AD. The Roman Emperor Caracalla was compelled to face them north of the river Main and defeated them, but this only temporarily held them back. Twenty years later, Alamanni warriors made a surprise attack on the eastern Raetian wall along the Danube frontier. They annihilated the Roman fort at present-day Pfunz. Archaeological evidence reinforces the suddenness of the attack. The charred skeletons of Roman guards have been found together in the guardroom with untouched shields nearby and scattered coins. Emperor Severus Alexander was forced back from campaigning in Persia to deal with these invaders, but such was the intrigue among his own officers, that he was compelled to bribe the Germans with gold rather than fighting them. This duplicity resulted in rioting and both the Emperor and his mother were killed, victims, some might say, of pressure brought to bear by the Alamanni.

The use of gold by the Romans to buy off the attacks of barbarians became a favourite defence which was raised to a pinnacle of strategy by the Byzantines who funded most of eastern Europe and its tribes with money raised from its wealthy trade routes running through Constantinople. Such a strategy, however, indicates that this was the time of the Late Roman Empire when its armed forces were no longer superior to the barbarians it encountered and that politics mattered as much as military might. It was also a sign of

weakness and one that the Alamanni were happy to exploit. Having battled with the Romans throughout the 250s, they finally broke through the frontier to raid deep into northern Italy. The Emperor's son Gallienus tracked them down near Milan and defeated them but they had already achieved something that only the Celts hundred of years before had tasted, entry into Roman Italy. Next came invasions of Gaul, where they joined with the Franks in their attacks on this wealthy province. Every time, the Romans managed to press the Alamanni back and reinforce their frontier fortifications but the new reality was clear that large German forces could wreak tremendous destruction on the Roman Empire and there was little the Roman army could do to stop them. The balance of power was beginning to shift in favour of the northern barbarians.

The painting depicts a scene in the 230s AD with Alamanni warriors leading a surprise attack on a Roman fort along the Danube frontier. Roman guards have been silenced and the German warriors creep silently inside the fortress walls. They wear primitive clothes associated with earlier German warriors, furs and simple tunics, but the helmet worn by the central warrior reveals their increasing military sophistication. This Spangenhelm with its hinged cheek-pieces, mail neck-guard, nasal, and conical cap made up of leaf-shaped segments of iron is a style of helmet indigenous to German warriors of the late Roman period (this particular one being similar to a helmet found at Morken in Germany and said to belong to a Frankish chieftain about 600 AD). The Spangenhelm remained popular among German warriors for hundreds of years and was adopted by the Romans themselves. All three warriors also carry another specifically Germanic piece of equipment—the francisko. With its curved axe-blade this was frequently used as a throwing axe alongside javelins and spears.

Burgundians enter southern France, 4th century AD

(Plate 9)

Anew realism gripped the administrators of the Roman Empire by the late 4th century AD. Confederations of German barbarian tribes were crucial players in the increasingly complicated balancing act of maintaining imperial rule. Employed directly as auxiliaries into the Roman army, barbarian warriors had been relatively easy to control, but as the power of barbarian warlords increased in the previous century, these independent groups demanded more control over their own affairs. A new deal had to be struck.

In return for maintaining security against other raiding barbarians and suppressing internal revolts by peasants, Roman landowners granted portions of their land to barbarian groups to treat as their own. This in turn established a new realism among barbarian warlords who up to this stage had treated Roman territory merely as something to loot and devastate. Now, barbarians were encouraged to look upon the land as their own and to join in a partnership with Roman landowners in maintaining its security. A further incentive to act responsibly was the fact that this land was granted tax free, but interestingly, barbarian warlords could see the value of maintaining a habit of tax collection and instructed their soldiers that any further pieces of land bought on the open market would not include this exemption. After all, a barbarian warlord could earn more money from efficient tax collection than pillaging and that included taxing his own warriors!

In this manner, several major barbarian confederations "invaded" the Roman Empire. In reality, the majority were invited and were quick to obtain legal entitlement to their land. As a result, barbarian tribes could be assured of staying on their land for centuries. In Roman France, the Franks moved into the northern estates, the Alans into the centre, the Burgundians established themselves in the south east, while the Visigoths later joined them after their adventures in Italy to settle in south-western France and Spain. The land settled by the Burgundians, centred on the Rhone valley and around Dijon, became known as Burgundy in the Middle Ages and remains today as the name of this region in France, giving some idea of the thoroughness with which the original Burgundii tribe established themselves on this territory.

Little is known about the Burgundians as no great saga of their early history has survived, unlike that of the Goths or the Franks. But that they were trusty supporters of the Roman Empire and their place within it is indicated by the fate of the only recorded early Burgundian warlord. Guntarius and his warriors fought alongside Aetius, the greatest of late Roman commanders, in his campaigns against the raiding Huns and was killed at one such battle in 436 AD.

The painting shows a warband of Burgundians leaving their mountainous homeland in central Europe to join in the barbarian settlement of Gaul in the late 4th century. The hexagonal shields betray a Celtic influence, which is not surprising considering their proximity to Celtic culture, and they may well have been a confederation of mixed Celtic and Germanic blood. The leading warrior also exhibits the impact of the Roman Empire, carrying both a Roman-style helmet and a Roman dagger, perhaps captured in border skirmishes with Roman soldiers. At his waist hangs a long, straight double-edged iron sword or spatha. Its narrow ornamented cross-guard recalls earlier Celtic swords, but it is characteristic of many such swords uncovered in 4th century burials. Before their settlement on Roman land, the Burgundians would have had less access to body armour and relied mainly on their shields, but as they drew on Roman wealth in the early 5th century, many of them would have joined the leading warrior here by wearing either scale or mail shirts. The dragon standard held by the second warrior is also typical of this period, being based on the windsock principal with wind passing through the dragon's mouth and inflating the body. Such standards were as popular among the Romans as among the barbarians and may ultimately have originated from the Sarmatian tribes of the Eurasian steppes.

(Plate 10)

The Franks were the descendants of those German tribes who had ambushed and massacred the Roman army of Valens in the dark forests west of the Rhine in 9 AD. Three centuries later they had grown even stronger and not lost any of their mastery of the land they inhabited. In a Roman counter-raid against the Franks in the 4th century, the historian Sulpicius Alexander tells how the Franks pretended to be scared and retreated further into the German forest. The Romans burnt their village and then pursued the Franks into a killing ground devised by the barbarians.

"By about midday, the Romans had lost themselves in a maze of pathways," records Sulpicius Alexander. "They ran up against an endless barricade solidly constructed from huge tree-trunks and then they tried to break out over the marshy fields which bordered the forest. Here and there barbarian troops showed themselves, standing on trees or climbing above the barricades as if on ramparts. They kept shooting arrows as if from catapults, and these they smeared with poisons distilled from plants, so that wounds which did little more than graze the skin and touched no vital organ were followed by death against which there was no protection."

Panicking and recoiling from one trap to another, the Romans stumbled out on to boggy open land where the Franks ran them down, spearing the soldiers caught in the mud. Some Romans rushed back in to the forest for cover, but were hunted down and the entire expedition was wiped out. On operations such as this the Franks built their fierce reputation and it is little wonder that by the end of the 4th century, the Romans had decided to incorporate them on their side of the Rhine as a defence against other barbarian tribes behind them.

Frankish warfare remained of a primitive style, best suited to forests, even after their settlement within the Roman Empire. "They have hardly any horsemen," wrote Agathias in the 6th century. "They bear swords and shields, but never use the sling or bow. Their missiles are axes and barbed javelins (angones). These last are not very long and can be used either to throw or to stab. The iron of the head runs so far down the shaft that very little of the wood remains unprotected. In battle they hurl these javelins, and if they strike an enemy, the barbs are so firmly fixed in this body that he cannot draw the weapon out. If it strikes a shield, it is impossible for him to get rid of it by cutting off the head for the iron runs too far down the shaft. At this moment the Frank rushes in, places his foot on the butt as it trails on the ground, and pulling the shield down, cleaves his unprotected foe through the head, or pierces his breast with a second spear." This use of the angon seems inspired by the Roman pilum. Agathias' assertion that the Franks never use bows is contradicted by the passage quoted previously, although the fact that the Franks may have been prejudiced against the bow is verified by Gregory of Tours in his 6th century History of the Franks, who describes a particularly loathsome warrior as being armed with a bow, thus establishing the preference of the later Western medieval knight for fighting with sword and lance rather than like oriental horse-archers.

The painting shows two Frankish warriors coming across a Roman soldier who has died from exposure. The nearest warrior is armed with the characteristic franciska axe while his companion carries the angon javelin with its long iron neck and barbed head. The emblematic importance of the axe in Frankish lore is perhaps best indicated by a story in which the early Frank King Clovis addresses a gathering of his warriors after a successful raid into the heart of Roman France. He declares that all the booty is to be divided equally, except for a sacred ewer, which he wishes to return to a bishop. One of his warriors resents this, however, and raises his franciska, slicing the vessel in half. Clovis hid his fury and delivered the broken relic to the bishop, but he later gathered all his warriors together to inspect their weaponry. Coming to the warrior who had denied him the sacred ewer, Clovis took away his sword, axe, and javelin, throwing them to the ground, saying they were in a poor condition for fighting. The warrior bent down to retrieve his weapons, but as he did so, Clovis drew his own axe and split the man's skull in two, just as the warrior had done to the one object he wanted.

Goths and Sarmatian, eastern Europe, 4th century AD

(Plate 11)

The grasslands north of the Black Sea and running into eastern Europe as far as present-day Hungary have been a road way for many of the Asian hordes that have terrorised Europe, from the Scythians to the Mongols. It is here too that several cultures have mingled and influenced each other. From the south came the Greeks and Byzantines, bringing their own trade and settled ways of life. From the north, from the lands surrounding the Baltic Sea, down the Great Russian rivers, have come numerous ways of German tribesmen. In the early centuries of the Christian era, these German settlers and raiders were known as Goths (they would later be called Vikings or Rus) and were divided into two main confederations called Ostrogoths ("eastern Goths") and Visigoths ("western Goths").

By the time the Goths arrived in the Crimea and surrounding areas the mighty culture of the Scythians appears to have been in decline and that of the Sarmatians was dominant. Possibly an Iranian-speaking people based in the northern Caucasus, the Sarmatians maintained the steppe culture of previous Eurasian barbarians and this included a warfare based around the horse, but unlike the Scythians who were mainly lightly clad horse-archers, the Sarmatians appear to have been given greater emphasis to the role of armoured horsemen armed with long lances, a style of fighting more akin to the Persians to the south of them. Archaeological and literary evidence suggests these warriors were clad in scale armour with iron helmets or, as Pausanias puts it: "anyone who has not seen a dragon is best advised to compare the appearance of a warrior clad in such armour to a green fir cone". The green perhaps referring to the tarnishing of bronze scales by exposure to air.

That the Sarmatian style of warfare influenced the Romans is without doubt and certainly the Goths, living nearest to them, must have been equally inspired and copied many of their traits. But the Goths managed also to maintain their own Germanic forms of warfare alongside them, thus creating a highly dynamic combination of foot and mounted warriors in one army. In later years, the Sarmatians appear to have been succeeded by the Alans, who dominated a similar part of the Black Sea region before joining the Goths in their migrations westwards. Even more than the Goths, the Alans combined both Sarmatian and German styles of warfare into one.

It was the appearance of the Huns in the 4th century AD, a Turkic confederation from central Asia near the Caspian Sea that brought the old Black Sea balance of power to an end, forcing both the Goths and their Sarmatian/Alan neighbours to move westwards bringing them into collision with the eastern Roman Empire. At first they came as refugees, bringing all their families and animals with them and the Romans were compelled to allow them to set up their camps on territory around the Danube frontier, but soon the Gothic warbands turned to raiding and looting the prosperous settlements of the Roman Balkans.

In 378 AD, the Emperor Valens decided to bring an end to this situation and marched towards the main Gothic encampment near Adrianople. Up until to this point, the Emperor had been commanding a successful guerrilla campaign against the ravaging Gothic bands, but against his best advice he wanted to finish it once and for all. His legionaries surrounded the wagon laager protecting the Gothic camp. It was a hot day and the Romans added to the discomfort of the Goths by lighting fires on the plain around the camp. Inside the wagon laager, the Goths had to play for time and proposed peace. As the Romans grew weary, a cloud of dust appeared behind them, joined by the thud of horses' hooves. A force of Goth horse-warriors had returned from their raiding and now ploughed into the unsuspecting Romans. Panic and chaos did the rest. Tightly packed between the Goth cavalry and the Goths, who now emerged from their wagons, the Roman army broke and in the pursuit almost two thirds of them were slaughtered, among them the Emperor Valens himself. It was a significant defeat for the forces of the Empire and heralded a new period of instability in which barbarian tribes rode throughout the eastern Empire.

The painting shows a meeting between a Sarmatian and two Goths in the forest of eastern Europe. They treat each other suspiciously. For much of their time on the steppe, they would have been enemies, raiding each other's territory, but now, in the wake of the Hun invasion of their land, they are now all refugees. Some Sarmatians would have fought alongside the Goths, but others might well have joined with the Hun horde. The Goths wear typically Germanic clothing, while the Sarmatian wears scale armour and iron helmet with cloak based on the marble stele found at the mouth of the river Don on the coast of the Sea of Azov in southern Russia.

(Plate 12)

Why is it that the Huns have endured as the most ferocious of all the barbarian tribes that rode through Roman frontiers? Other tribes were notorious for barbaric practices, such as the Alani, stripping the skin off their enemies to use as saddle cloths, and others were certainly more successful—the Huns never secured a kingdom for themselves in the remains of the Empire, although the land of Hungary does still bear their name. Part of the reason lies in the use made of their name over the centuries and most recently, in the early part of the 20th century, when Kaiser William II, executor of the First World War, gave it an extra spin. In the summer of 1900, the Kaiser saw off an expeditionary force to China to quell the Boxer rebellion. In a speech to his soldiers he proclaimed: "Just as the Huns under their King, Attila, a thousand years ago made for themselves a name which men still respect, so should you give the name of German such reason to be remembered in China for a thousand years that no Chinaman shall dare to look a German in the face." On this occasion, the Germans failed, but under Hitler they would achieve the reputation for barbarity the Kaiser so eagerly recommended. As a direct result of this speech, however, Germans in the First World War were nicknamed "Huns" by their British adversaries.

The other reason for the notoriety of the Huns is, of course, Attila, their most famous leader. He has been portrayed as a demonic figure over the centuries. Our most reliable descriptions of him come from Priscus, a Roman ambassador who travelled to Attila's camp and gives us an eyewitness account of what he saw. Immediately, we are aware that this is no tinpot leader trying to impress with his own greedily acquired power and riches, but a man aware only of his authority and position within the tribe. Priscus describes the warlord at a feast held in honour of the Romans: "While sumptuous food had been prepared and was served on silver dishes for the other barbarians and for us, for Attila there was nothing but meat on a wooden plate. He showed himself restrained in all other ways too, for gold and silver goblets were offered to the men at the feast, but his cup was of wood. His dress was plain, caring for nothing but to be clean, no sword at his side, neither were the clasps on his barbarian boots or the bridle of his horse like those of other Scythians adorned with gold or precious gems." While the others laughed at entertainers, Attila was unmoved, smiling only when his young son approached him. It is easy to see why a man such as this should command such reverence among his men.

Attila became king of the Huns by murdering his brother, Bleda,

in 445 AD. He was probably of Turkic origin, although there are eastern German sounding names recorded in his family and certainly by this time, the Huns were a confederation of tribes that included both Turkic and Gothic warriors. Attila now continues to be a hugely popular name in eastern Europe where he is regarded more as a hero than a villain. For almost a decade, Attila and his Huns made their name and their wealth by plundering the eastern Roman Empire, frequently being bought off by enormous bribes by the Byzantine government. In 450 AD, he decided to try his luck against the western Roman Empire, but this was where he came unstuck. He even hoped to marry the sister of the western Roman Emperor and thus legally inherit half of the Roman dominion, but neither the Romans nor the Visigoths who already dominated much of the western Empire would be so easily shifted.

In 451 AD at the so-called battle of Chalons, Attila was soundly stopped by a combined Roman and barbarian force. This deflected him from the rich lands of Gaul and he sought instead some recompense in northern Italy, but he failed to reach Rome and had to withdraw because of threats to his eastern realms. Shortly afterwards, he died famously from a nose-bleed caused by celebrating the addition of a new wife to his harem, although this runs contrary to the sober character depicted by Priscus. Maybe rivals emboldened by his failures in western Europe poisoned him instead. Internecine strife followed his death and the Huns never again regained the power and reputation they had under Attila, although they continued as a military force, frequently being hired by their Roman foes.

The painting shows Attila receiving a tribute from a Chinese envoy in the form of treasure and women. It may be that the envoy represents the interests of Chinese merchants wanting protected access to the lucrative central Asian trade route over which Attila may have had some influence, although his ambitions were mainly westwards into Europe.

Death of Theoderic, king of the Visigoths, battle of Chalons, 451 AD

(Plate 13)

The battle of Chalons was one of the great combats of the Barbarian era. Just as the battle of Adrianople marked the entrance of the barbarians into the Roman Empire as an empire-shaking force in the late 4th century, so, almost eighty years later, the battle of Chalons symbolised the high-water mark of the eastern steppe-warriors. After 451 AD, the Turkic tribes of Attila never stood a chance of dominating what remained of the western Roman Empire, this would be divided between the victors of that day—the Germanic tribes and their late Roman allies. Indeed, the alliance between Roman and German on that day goes some way to explain the transition from Roman Empire to Germanic Kingdom. Both factions saw the need to preserve the prosperity of Western European culture against the looting and ravaging of steppe raiders.

The battle of Chalons is itself a misnomer. A hundred years ago, Thomas Hodgkin devoted many words to proving that among the ancient sources it seems likely that the battle was actually fought near Troyes in northern France. Attila, warlord of the Huns, had broken his usual pattern of raiding the eastern Roman Empire to test the will of the west and crossed the Rhine leading a considerable army of Turkic and Germanic warriors. In his way stood those Germanic tribes who had already fought their way into Gaul, principally the Visigoths led by Theoderic, and Aetius, a half-barbarian, half-Roman warlord who represented the concerns of late Roman landowners. For his role in this battle, Aetius has been called the last of the Romans, but it was his time spent as an official hostage among the Huns that equipped him best for this confrontation. As a man in his 20s, he found the life of the Huns exhilarating, becoming a "superb horseman, a fine shot with an arrow and tireless with the lance," according to the chronicler Renatus Frigeridus. "He scorned danger and was able to endure hunger, thirst and loss of sleep." This hardness made him a favourite among his soldiers. At Chalons, however, he was in his 60s and experience would have to be his guide. In this, he was matched by the Visigothic king Theoderic, a senior chieftain among his warriors who had used his skills of negotiation and politics as much as warfare to secure tight control over vast estates in Gaul.

It was Attila who was the new kid on the block, determined to build on his successful raids in the east to secure his own estates in the prosperous west. Gaul, however, would prove to be a harder nut to crack. Jordanes, a Romanised Goth, is our major source for this encounter and he describes it in titanic terms. Attila seems, surprisingly, to have been influenced by the bad omens read in sheep intestines by his shamen to delay the fight until the afternoon. The battlefield centred on a slope with both sides riding to gain the advantage of the height. The Roman-German army consisted of Theoderic and his Visigoths on the right flank, Aetius and his Romans on the left, and Sangiban and his Alans in the centre, being the least dependable of the allied forces. The line of the Huns was drawn up with Attila in the centre surrounded by his most loyal troops with his Germanic allies on the flanks, including the Ostrogoths and Gepidae. It was a battle fought mainly by horsemen, wielding either lances or swords if they were Germanic, or bows and spears if they were Roman or Huns. Aetius and his allies claimed the height of the ridge first and the Huns retreated in confusion.

Like a Caesar, Attila was forced to ride among his men and rally them with a speech. "Let the wounded exact in vengeance the death of his foe," he bellowed. "Let those without wounds revel in the slaughter of the enemy! No spear shall harm those who are destined to live. And those who are sure to die, fate overtakes anyway in peace!" Of course, these are the words of the chronicler, but no doubt based on the fact that Attila's presence proved crucial in holding his troops on the battlefield. Both Theoderic and Aetius chose also to be at the heart of the battle and it was at this moment that the Visigothic king fell from his horse, not to rise again. His warriors were distraught, but rather than being broken, they used their anger to give them the extra strength needed to force the Huns back on to their camp. Many of Attila's allies fled, but the Hun king would not leave his loot and as darkness fell he turned his camp into a fort. The Visigoths swore to annihilate the Huns and Attila began to burn many of his wagons in preparation for the final assault, but Aetius managed to persuade the Germans to let the Hun go. A wounded lion is always more dangerous and the Visigoths were themselves without a leader and as such vulnerable, so Attila was allowed to retreat, but never again would he threaten the west.

Vandal and Alan warriors in North Africa, 5th century AD

(Plate 14)

The Vandals achieved perhaps the greatest barbarian migration of them all. From their homeland in eastern Europe, they trekked through France and Spain, fighting all the way against Romans and barbarian competitors, to end up in North Africa where they carved out a substantial kingdom that lasted a century before Belasarius, the great Byzantine commander, finally defeated them. In the meantime, they sacked the city of Rome in 455 AD and acquired a reputation for destruction which endures today. Procopius, the greatest chronicler of the Vandals, describes them as Germanic in origin. "The greatest names of this alliance of nations," he wrote, "are Goth and Vandal and Visigoth and Gepid. They all have fair skins and yellow hair, are tall of stature and handsome to look upon. They all possess the same laws, the same faith of Arian Christianity, and the same Gothic language. To me they appear all to have formed part of one nation in ancient times and afterwards to have been distinguished from each other by the names of their leaders." What on earth the dark skinned natives of North Africa made of these blond, giant warriors when they rode ashore from their boats is anybody's guess.

Gaiseric was the greatest of the Vandal leaders. Like Attila, he possessed a reputation as a serious ruler. "He was a man of deep thought and few words," wrote Jordanes, "holding luxury in disdain, furious in his anger, greedy for gain, shrewd in winning over the barbarians and skilled in sowing the seeds of discord among his enemies." Despite being a bastard son of the king of the Vandals, his reputation enabled him to push aside the legitimate heir and he became king sometime before 429 AD. Having been denied land in France and finding little respite in Spain from the Romans and their Visigoth allies, Gaiseric saw an opportunity for settled land in the Roman provinces of North Africa. A riding accident had left him lame but he still commanded the respect of his people and he suggested they use their control of ports in southern Spain to launch an invasion of Africa. The Alani, a tribe of Turkic warriors from the Black Sea, who had ridden with them throughout their earlier quests, joined them in this adventure. They were also joined no doubt by Moorish and Spanish sailors and adventurers who also saw great opportunities and perhaps provided the maritime expertise needed for this expedition.

Fortunately for Gaiseric, the defence of Roman North Africa was in the hands of Boniface, a once effective warlord who was plagued by his own inner doubts about whether he should give up his bloody career and become a monk. Shaken by the appearance of two Roman armies sent to replace him, it appears Boniface may even have invited the Vandals across the sea to help him maintain his position. Whatever the truth, there was political weakness in North Africa which Gaiseric decisively exploited, landing with perhaps as many as 80,000 warriors. Almost immediately, a religious civil war began in which the Arian Vandals vanquished the native Catholics and laid waste their churches, thus forever ensuring their name became a byword for wanton destruction. Boniface was defeated and Gaiseric recognised as the lawful ruler of North Africa. This recognition by Rome did not stop the vandals from exploiting their ownership of key African ports to now establish a reputation as formidable pirates, raiding fleets and ports throughout the Mediterranean. The most celebrated pirate raid was on Rome. For two weeks, Gaiseric resided in the palace of the Emperor, making the Imperial family his prisoners and all the riches of Rome his own. The Roman government was in no state to oppose him, but rather than proclaim himself Emperor, Gaiseric merely sailed back to Carthage, his reputation and coffers enormously enhanced.

The entire original Vandal and Alani that accompanied Gaiseric to Africa were now rich beyond their wildest dreams. Sidonius claims this luxury effected Gaiseric: "Thanks to untold gold, he no longer knows aught of steel. A drunkard's heaviness afflicts him, pallid flabbiness possesses him, and his stomach, loaded with continual gluttony cannot rid itself of the sour wind." This is more wishful thinking among the Romans and Gaiseric's vigorous leadership continued for decades, but the composition of his army was transformed. As the original barbarians retired to their estates, the majority of the Vandal army was composed of North African Moorish tribesmen. They rode camels and incorporated their animals in spear phalanxes, which sometimes disturbed horses sent against them. The warriors depicted in the painting, however, are from the earlier period of conquest, showing both a Germanic Vandal in mail shirt and a Turkic Alan in eastern influenced lamella armour.

Saxon warriors, southern England, 6th century AD

(Plate 15)

The Saxons were the last great Germanic confederation to grab a piece of the Roman Empire. Rather than marching southwards from their homelands in the Netherlands and Denmark, they sailed across the English Channel to raid and then settle in Roman Britain. Recruited as auxiliaries in the Roman British army, they were used to life within Britain and when the last official Roman governors withdrew from the island at the beginning of the 5th century, their presence increased until they considered it their realm. At first they took control of the lands that still bear their names today, such as Essex and Sussex in south-east England, but then they moved westwards and clashed with the Romano-Celtic warlords of southern and western England. The most famous of these clashes was with the Romano-British warlord now known as Arthur, who later became the central figure of a celebrated cycle of medieval tales featuring Camelot and knights such as Lancelot. The original Arthur, however, wore not shining armour, but quasi-Roman armour, perhaps featuring a mail shirt or shirt of iron scales.

The real Camelot may well have been the Roman fortress of Caeleon in south Wales, whose arena may have been the inspiration behind the celebrated Knights of the Round Table. A string of battles between Arthur and the Saxons is recorded by Nennius who has the war culminating at the battle of Badon Hill. Nennius describes the hot water that bubbled up at the natural springs of Badon and this seems to suggest a location at the Roman settlement of Bath with its natural hot water bathing complex. The chroniclers agree that it took place over three days and thus may have involved a siege of the Roman town. The end was precipitated by a great cavalry charge by Arthur who swept the Saxons off the field and kept them out of the West Country for several decades. The weight of history, however, was with the Saxons and by the 8th century, they dominated most of England, forcing the Celts to the outlying lands that still remain today largely Celtic in character.

The painting shows three richly clad Saxon warriors, either warlords themselves or senior warriors closely attached to their commanders. They wear the very pinnacle of British Dark Ages arms and armour, based on the famous find at Sutton Hoo in which the grave of a warlord was discovered beneath a mound lying in the remains of a Saxon ship—this is a classic Viking-style burial in which a lord is laid to rest in the vehicle of his conquests and indeed reflects many close parallels between the military culture of the Saxons and the Vikings who followed them. The most glorious aspect of this find is the helmet (worn by the central figure in the painting) which is of the crested Ridge-type, closely related to late Roman military helmets, consisting of an iron bowl fixed to a metal crest with cheek and neck guards hung from the crest. The iron surface is covered with thin copper alloy plates stamped with intricate motifs. The distinctive eye guards are cast from bronze and terminate in stylised boar heads. The face guard is constructed of iron with nose, mouth, and moustache features applied to it. The figure on the left wears a helmet based on one recently discovered at Coppergate in York. Also of the Ridge-type construction, it features iron nasal and cheek guards. Mail was frequently added to such helmets to form a neckguard or, as in the figure on the right, to create a veil protecting the face.

The weapon characteristic of the Saxons and from which they may have derived their name, was the seax. A long single-edged knife, almost a short sword, it was intended as a battle weapon, perhaps used by men carrying spears who needed it for close combat. Saxon swords are splendid implements. The sword found at Sutton Hoo has a pattern-welded blade. This was a process evolved when good quality steel was in short supply, smiths making blades out of a combination of light case-hardened iron and darker softer iron. The alternating layers of metal were sandwiched together, twisted and welded into one piece. Cutting edges of steel were separately welded onto this core. Half the total weight was then removed through grinding and the cutting edge filed. Finally, the blades were treated with an acid, anything form urine to sour beer, and the wavy pattern on the blade resulting from the sandwich of different irons was highlighted with etching and polishing. These patterns were much admired and gave rise to nicknames for swords such as "Fishback" or "Dragonsword".

Angus McBride '98

Avar and Bulgar warriors, eastern Europe, 8th century AD

(Plate 16)

In the power vacuum left by the death of Attila and the warfare between his successors, rode a new confederation of steppe warriors—the Avars. Like the Huns, they were of Turkic origin, and included many of the descendants of the warriors that rode with Attila. Indeed, so closely were they associated with the Huns that this is the name by which they were called by many western European chroniclers. From the 6th century onwards they raided and plundered the eastern Roman Empire and, unlike Attila's horde, did not become too ambitious so as to wreck their achievements, dominating central Europe for almost three centuries, only running out of steam when they clashed with the resurgent power of the Franks under Charlemagne.

The war against Charlemagne was a bitter war one lasting some eight years, the Frankish chronicler Einhard describing it as an absolute victory for the Franks: "Just how many battles were fought and how much blood was shed is shown by the fact that Pannonia (the name of the old Roman province where they lived) is now completely uninhabited and that the site of the Khan's palace is now so deserted that no evidence remains that anyone ever lived there. All the Avar nobility died in this war, all their glory departed. All their wealth and their treasures assembled over so many years were dispersed." The completeness of this victory is certainly over-emphasised to suit the taste of the Carolingian court, but the defeat undoubtedly left room for other later tribes to prosper, such as the Magyars. But at the height of their power, the Avars were almost unassailable, diverting much of the wealth of Byzantium into their own coffers through either ransom or raiding. They subdued the Slavs that followed the Germanic tribes into the Balkans and central Europe, treating them as a lower caste, sleeping with their women, expecting tribute from their men, using them as footsoldiers to fight in the frontlines of their armies to blunt enemy opposition. Eventually, the Slavs rose in rebellion and threw off their domination by the Avars.

The Avars fought much as the Huns fought, employing horse-archers to harass and exhaust their enemies and then closing with more heavily armed and armoured horsemen. In his manual of military tactics and organisation, the Byzantine Emperor Maurice describes their typical fighting methods: "They prefer battles fought at long range, ambushes, encircling their enemies, faking retreats with sudden returns, and wedge-shaped formations of loose groups. When they make their adversaries take to flight, they put everything aside and, unlike the Romans, Persians, and other races, who pursue only a reasonable distance and plunder their goods, the Avars do not give up until they have achieved the complete destruction of their enemies." In other words, they used typical nomadic raiding tactics, but with a meaner edge. A political faction within Constantinople, based on the hippodrome street gangs known as the Blues, are believed to have copied the appearance of the Avar which included hair shorn on the front of the scalp but left to grow long at the back, full tunics that were belted tightly at the waist but spread out to the shoulders, capes, trousers and boots typical of steppe warriors.

The decline of the power of the Avars in the 9th century allowed the Bulgars to exercise more power in eastern Europe. Another confederation of steppe tribesmen, they had settled to the south of the Avars in the Balkans and the land of Bulgaria still bears their name. Their greatest moment of military success came in 811 AD when the Byzantine Emperor Nicephorus marched against them. Initially, the Byzantines plunged deep into Bulgar territory and burnt their capital, but the Bulgars struck back with a surprise attack on the Byzantine encampment and Nicephorus was killed, his skull being turned into a drinking goblet in true Scythian style. They even tried to storm Constantinople, but could not breach its massive walls, and the Byzantines wrought a devastating revenge on them. A Bulgar army was defeated by Basil II who had every Bulgar prisoner blinded, except for every hundredth warrior who was left with one eye so he could lead his humbled comrades back to the land they came from.

The painting shows an Avar and Bulgar warrior, both wearing Turkic style armour and eastern influenced weapons, including a composite bow and scimitar.

Lombard warriors, northern Italy, 8th century AD

(Plate 17)

The Lombards or Langobardi (their name means "long beards") were one of the last Germanic confederations to invade Roman Italy. Throughout the turmoil of the 5th century when the western Roman Empire was finally toppled by the Goths, they remained in their homeland along the Danube, but with the resurgence of Roman power in the 6th century under the eastern Roman Emperor Justinian and his general Narses, the Lombards were called upon to help the Romans in their reconquest of Gothic Italy. It was a bitter war that dragged on for many years with both sides gaining and losing battles, but eventually it was the Goths who provided less resistant and their hold on Italy was shattered.

As Narses and his eastern Roman warriors returned to Constantinople, the Lombards saw their chance. In 568 AD, the Lombards poured into northern Italy. Unable to shift the Byzantines from their coastal trading realms, they nevertheless carved out several dukedoms for their warlords and such was their impact that this region of Italy still bears their name and is known as Lombardy. They were there two hundred years later when the Pope in Rome complained to Charlemagne about their raiding and the great Frankish warlord was forced to react. The Lombards maintained the barbaric character of their German neighbours and their king was said to drink from the skull of his greatest enemy. That the Lombards actually enjoyed this kind of reputation is demonstrated when Paul the Deacon, a Lombard himself, wrote the history of his people in the 7th century and included a reference to the notorious cup: "I speak the truth in Christ. I saw King Ratchis holding this cup in his hand on a certain festal day, to show it to his friends." By then, of course, the Lombards had adopted many of the more civilised ways of the Romans, including Christianity.

In the 6th century, the Lombards were armed similarly to the Franks, using both stabbing and throwing spears, as well as throwing axes. They were renowned as horsemen, bringing a great interest in horse breeding and riding to their realms in northern Italy. As horsemen they fought with lances and long swords and one contemporary account describes a Lombard champion lifting a Byzantine soldier high in the air on the end of his lance. The Franks were later to take to this kind of warfare and in these German horse-warriors, clad in armour with sword and lance, we see the birth of the medieval knight that was to dominate western Europe for the next thousand years. Like knights too, they decorated their round wooden shields with images of Christ, Christian symbols, and crosses.

In the 770s, Charlemagne, who had carved out a massive Frankish realm in France, invaded northern Italy. He had married the daughter of the King of the Lombards and considered this his claim to their throne, but when the woman died, her Lombard father rose in revolt. Charlemagne's armoured presence in the lands of the Lombards, surrounded by armoured knights, excited a contemporary chronicler: "Then came in sight that man of iron, Charlemagne, topped with his iron helm, his fists in iron gloves, his iron chest and his shoulders clad in an iron cuirass. An iron spear raised high against the sky he gripped in his left hand, while in his right he held his still unconquered sword. For greater ease of riding other men keep their thighs bare of armour; Charlemagne's were bound in plates of iron." Despite this impressive battlefield appearance, the main combat revolved around a siege of Pavia in which the Lombards were forced to admit Charlemagne's supremacy.

The painting depicts a scene during Charlemagne's campaign in which Lombards have dispatched one of the ironclad Frankish invaders. The main Lombard warrior wears a spangenhelm with body armour made of lamella, a kind of scale armour adopted by the Romans from the Middle East. Lamella consisted of long narrow iron scales laced both horizontally and vertically and because of this lacing needed no leather backing, unlike the more traditional scale armour worn by the dead Frank which was attached to fabric or leather and so was less flexible and vulnerable to upward thrusts.

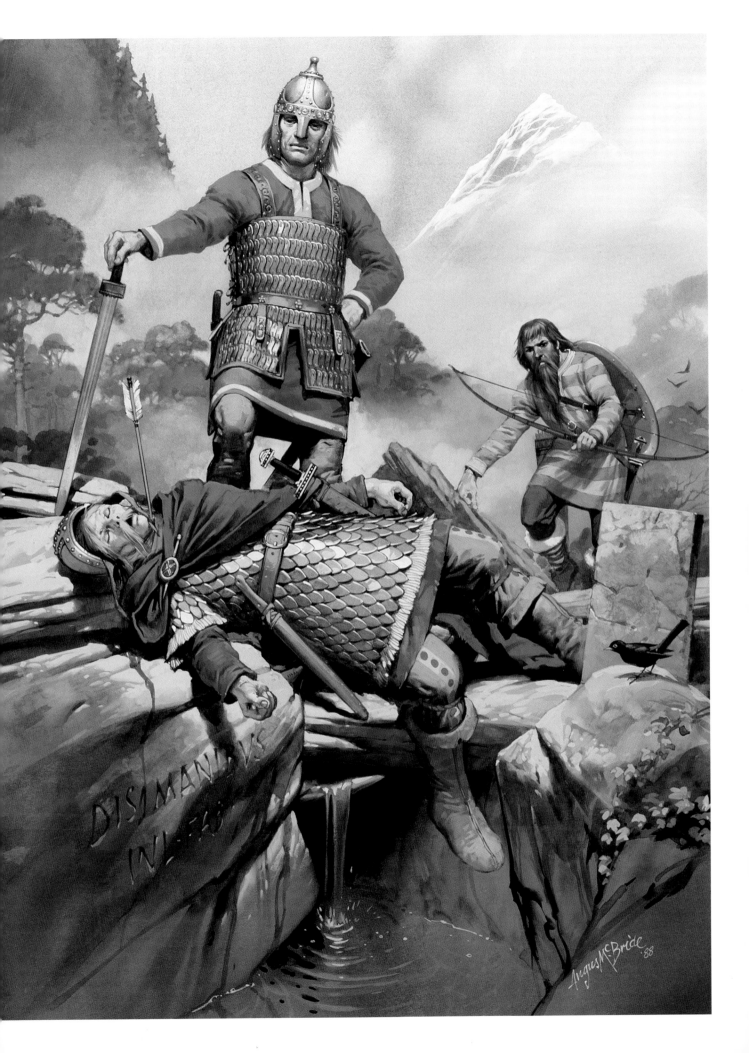

Viking raiders clash with Carolingians near Paris, 9th century AD

(Plate 18)

At first, it was the Vikings who had most to fear from the Carolingians. Charlemagne had forced his dominion northwards from his French heartland into the land of the Saxons in the present-day Netherlands, slaughtering 4,500 of these heathens in just one day. To Charlemagne, it was a Christian crusade, in which the northern barbarians were to be treated as sub-humans. According to the chronicler Notka, Charlemagne had a simple test for any captured Northmen: "He ordered all their boys and children to be measured by the sword, that is, any who exceeded such a measurement were shortened by a head." In response to this, the King of the Danes had a massive earthwork built, linking the North Sea to the Baltic. Behind this defensive line, he then planned a 200-ship raid which shook Carolingian control of Frisia, but with the death of both kings the conflict subsided. It was only a temporary respite and by the middle of the 9th century, it was the turn of the Vikings to invade French territory.

The raids began along the coast, but as their influence grew stronger and French resistance was swapped for protection money, the Vikings launched boat-borne campaigns along the great rivers of France. In the wake of Charlemagne, the Carolingian dynasty was proving weak and many local French landowners allied themselves with the Vikings, seeing them as the ascendant power. Stealing or acquiring horses, the Vikings left their boats to strike deep inland. It did not help France that Alfred the Great was having more success against the Danes in England and thus was forcing them back to softer targets on the continent. In 885 AD, a huge Danish army sailed along the Seine to reach Paris, at this time sited around a fort on an island in the middle of the river. The Vikings immediately assaulted its stone and wood defences, but the Parisians were in no mood to surrender and hurled boiling oil, wax and pitch on them. Screaming and tearing at their burning hair, the Vikings plunged into the river and their commander, Count Eudes, settled for a siege.

The Vikings showed a great skill for siege warfare, creating battering rams, screens to shield archers, and catapults to throw lumps of molten lead into the city. But when the engines were pushed against the walls, the Parisian replied with equal ingenuity, dropping heavy beams wrapped in iron and firing arrows from <u>ballistae</u> mounted on the battlements. The siege continued for almost a year and in that time the Vikings tried everything, including sending blazing fire ships against the wooden bridges that linked the town to the mainland. Even relieving armies were fought off by the Danes, but still to no avail. Eventually, the Vikings had to settle for

tribute organised by the French king and Paris was left unconquered. In the long term, however, many Danes settled in northern France and these Northmen became the Normans of later generations.

The painting shows a clash between Viking raiders and Carolingian horsemen, the Vikings being caught as they disembark from their boats along the Seine. The Carolingian horsemen are well equipped with late-Roman-style body armour of iron scales, based on illustrations in contemporary Carolingian manuscripts. Much was made of the Carolingian possession of iron armour by their own chroniclers, perhaps as a sign that they were both militarily and materially superior to the northern barbarians. One of their kings took a sword sent as tribute and, according to Notker, "tried to bend it from its tip to its handle. His hands were stronger than the sword and the blade snapped." In truth, the Vikings were very well equipped in both armour and weapons and their successful conquests in France proved they were the superior warriors, despite the reputation of Charlemagne and his elite horsemen. The leading Viking warrior in the centre wears a helmet with eye-guards based on the Gjermundbhu remnants found in Norway. It is closely related to the <u>spangenhelm</u> in construction and could have had a veil of mail attached to its back.

Viking warriors, Norway, 10th century AD

(Plate 19)

The Vikings of Norway were perhaps the furthest travelled of all the Scandinavian warriors of the 9th and 10th centuries. Whereas the Danes merely hopped across the North Sea to eastern Britain where they enjoyed their greatest success, Norse ships took them across the ocean to the islands of Scotland and to Ireland. Further north, the Norwegians sailed to Iceland and Greenland and then onto North America where recent archaeological evidence gives greater credence to their claims of discovery and habitation of Vinland as they called this new continent. Their travels are perhaps only matched by the Swedes who turned eastwards, travelling the great rivers of Russia to arrive in the Black Sea and the Mediterranean. Relics of Arab coins and vessels discovered in Scandinavia suggest also that Vikings made contacts with the great trade routes of central Asia, making them one of the earliest peoples to establish a truly global trade network stretching from North America to China.

In their adventures westward, the Norwegians clashed with many indigenous peoples they called Scraelings. These were the Inuits of Canada and further along the American coast were Point Revenge Indians. Essentially stone-age peoples, they wore seal skins, armour of bark, flung flint-tipped arrows and spears, and rowed in wooden canoes or kayaks. Their numbers made up for their lack of technology and appear to have eventually worn down the presence of the Vikings in North America. By the 13th century, Eskimos had developed to the point where they were now expanding and chasing the Vikings out of their settlements in Greenland. Unlike the conquistadors of later centuries, the Norse Vikings appear not to have made the most of their military technological edge over these natives, perhaps because it was not great enough or because their numbers were not sufficient to outweigh the native warbands.

The Norwegian Vikings in the painting show the full extent of their military arsenal. Like their earlier southern German neighbours, the Vikings depended on mail armour, iron helmets, and shields for their defence. The distinctly Viking-style helmet on the warrior on the left is based on that found at Gjermundbu in Norway. Analysis of the remains of this helmet show that it comprised four external uprights riveted to four internal uprights which held in place four iron segments to which was riveted the brow band which also supported the eye guards. To this basic sound structure could be added a veil of mail, thus covering the entire face.

The iron sword and spear remained the favourite weapons of the Vikings with the addition of the typically Scandinavian long handled battleaxe wielded in two hands. This fierce looking weapon engendered many stories of superhuman ability, such as when Skarphedin Njalsson leapt from his boat only to land on ice and slide so quickly towards his enemy that the axe sliced into his head and "spilt his back teeth onto the ice". The double-handed battleaxe enjoyed its greatest reputation among the Viking-originating warrior employed in the Saxon army of King Harold who formed a formidable part of his shield wall against the Normans at Hastings in 1066. It also strongly influenced the Irish and Scots who devised their own versions of it. Archery was popular among the Vikings but because the bows were essentially simple wooden weapons, they could not compete with the stronger, more powerful composite bows of their Eurasian neighbours.

(Plate 20)

Hungary is a land of grassy plains surrounded by mountains. It is the very western end of the great Eurasian steppe land that stretches from central Europe all the way to northern China. Its name derives from some of it most famous inhabitants—the Huns. It was on this land that Attila and his hordes launched their raids on the decaying Roman Empire. Here was the pastureland for raising the horses that were such a vital part of their war machine. But what happened to the Huns after the death of Attila and the collapse of the Roman Empire?

Modern historians say the Huns just disappeared, overwhelmed by later invaders. Contemporary historians of the Dark Ages take a different view. They describe Huns as surviving into the 7th, 8th, and 9th centuries, giving that name to the hordes of Turkic invaders we now call Avars, Bulgars, and Pechenegs. Hungarians today refer to a people called the Szekely who live in Transylvania, barely half a million of them and these are believed to be the descendants of the last remaining Huns in central Europe. The name by which they live, however, is spoken in a language alien to the Turkic tongue of the Huns. It is Finno-Ugric and it is the language of the last great steppe warriors to settle in central Europe—the Magyars. So successful was this invasion of horse-borne warriors that today, a thousand years later, over 90 per cent of Hungarians still call themselves Magyars.

What is also most remarkable about the Magyars is that these tribesmen broke the thousand year cultural shift of Turkic and Germanic barbarians into Hungary and replaced it with a culture coming from the north, from the land east of the Baltic Sea, bringing them closer in cultural style to the Finns as well as the Lithuanians, Latvians, and Slavs. We therefore see warriors who were fine horsemen skilled with the composite bow, but also keen to fight in armour with sword and lance like western warriors. Their entry into Hungary was proclaimed in the 10th century. Prior to this they had clashed with the Rus and Bulgars in Russia and eastern Europe. When they arrived in Hungary, the great khanate of the Avars—or, the last of the Huns—had been fatally weakened by the Carolingians and Slavs around them, and they swiftly took over their role as raiders of central Europe.

One of the most ambitious of these raiding campaigns was their invasion of Italy. "No man ever wished more desperately for food or water than these savages desire a fight," wrote a chronicler of the action. "They scar their babies with knives so that they might bear the pain of wounds before receiving milk from their mothers' breasts." The Magyars crossed through the mountain passes of the Alps and sacked the wealthy towns of northern Italy. Their citizens'

defence was in the hands of the Carolingians and these armoured warriors rode to the attack. Initially, the Magyars retreated before them, like typical steppe warriors, preferring easy looting to hard fighting. They even offered to return much of their booty and prisoners, but the Carolingian Italians were sure of victory and forced the Magyars to battle. With nothing to lose, the Magyars took the offensive and surprised the majority of the Italians while they were resting and eating. It was a bitter slaughter with the Magyars wiping out their enemy so as to ensure a safe return to their land.

The news was no better for the rest in Germany where the Magyars thrashed the Carolingian king of their central European territories at Augsburg. Again, attacking before daybreak, the Magyars transfixed the Germans with their arrows and cut them down with their sabres. Much of western Europe was now vulnerable to repeated raids and the Magyars grew rich and powerful on their loot. In 955 AD, the biggest Magyar horde yet invaded the German states. This time, they lay siege to Augsburg, but as the Magyars strengthened their grip on the city, an army raised by Otto of Saxony arrived. Near the river Lech, a tributary of the Danube, the Christian Germans advanced against the pagan Magyars. In steppe warrior's style, the Magyars immediately sent a group of horsemen to attack the German baggage train and ravage their rearguard. Disaster seemed to have struck Otto almost immediately. Dispatching Duke Conrad to rally his rearguard troops, Otto concentrated on bringing the Magyars into close combat. An arrow struck Conrad to the ground, but Otto and his Germans kept up their assault with swords and lances and the Magyars finally gave ground. The retreat turned into a rout and the Magyars were hunted for two days, some being surrounded in village huts and burned alive. Never again would the Magyars venture into western Europe, but they were more than happy to remain in Hungary where they increasingly adopted the ways of their western neighbours, so that Hungarian/Magyar knights were among the toughest defenders of Christianity when the Ottoman Turks came to their land 500 years later.

The painting shows a typical Magyar raid of the early 10th century on a German settlement in central Europe. Both mounted warriors are heavily armed and armoured, demonstrating a particularly Magyar combination of fighting styles, making them closer to the Lithuanians and Poles than Turkic steppe tribesmen. Eastern influence, however, is clear in their composite bows, curved swords, and use of bird and feather emblems. Their mail armour and iron helmets are more western orientated.

Barbarian Arms and Armour

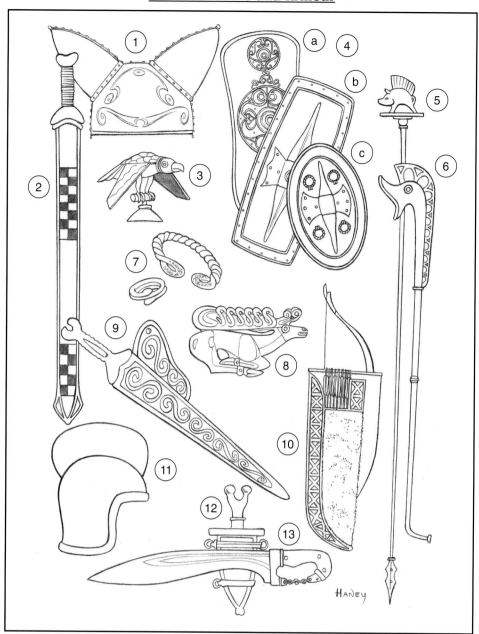

Today, it is very much assumed that less well developed cultures will be overwhelmed by the styles and objects of their modern neighbours, but in the ancient world, so-called barbarian cultures were very dominant and strong influences on the settled civilisations to the south of them. Perhaps the most influential barbarian culture was that of the Celts which helped transform Roman military culture from one copying the Greeks to a method of shield and sword warfare which eventually conquered most of Europe.

Drawings 1 and 3 show the highly decorative helmets and crests worn by Celtic warriors in the 1st and 2nd centuries BC. Some historians claim these are ceremonial, but we have enough contemporary literary descriptions from the Romans and Greeks to suggest that ornamented helmets were worn into battle, especially with animal crests. Drawing 2 is a splendid Celtic iron sword of the 1st century BC with typical sloping-shoulder guard on the hilt. Drawing 4 shows three Celtic shields ranging from the 2nd century BC (a) to the 1st century BC (b and c). Large rectangular and oval shields were a characteristic aspect of Celtic fighting skills and may well have influenced the adoption of such large body-protecting shields by the Romans. The Celts were renowned horsemen and their cavalry frequently featured as mercenaries in ancient Greek and Roman armies. Drawing 5 is a Celtic cavalry standard of the 1st century BC featuring a bronze boar, a symbol of strength. Drawing 6 is a Celtic war trumpet or carnyx of the 1st century BC. Drawing 7 shows both a Celtic torc, worn round the neck, and a bracelet, both of electrum

from the 2nd century BC. Worn by Celtic warriors in most sculptural representations of them, it is thought the torc was a sign of a free man, perhaps deriving from the symbolism of the rope noose usually worn round a captured slave that had been broken.

The other great pre-Christian barbarian culture to impact on Europe was that of the steppe peoples from southern Russia, around the Black Sea. Drawing 8 shows a Scythian shield ornament of gold of the 6th century BC. It is typical of nomadic culture in that it chooses animal imagery, in this case a deer with elaborated antlers. Drawing 9 is a Scythian sword and scabbard of the 5th century BC, while drawing 10 shows the more typical weapon of these horsemen, a combined quiver and bow case of the 4th century BC.

In Spain, where the invading Celts combined with the native culture of the Iberian people, it produced a martial mix that proved highly effective, giving the Romans one of the hardest fought wars of their military history. Typical of this ferocious conflict was the falcata, shown in drawing 13, a Celto-Iberian slashing sword that terrified its Roman opponents. Also typically Celto-Iberian are the crested helmet in drawing 11 and the triangular dagger in drawing 12, all these objects coming from the 2nd century BC.

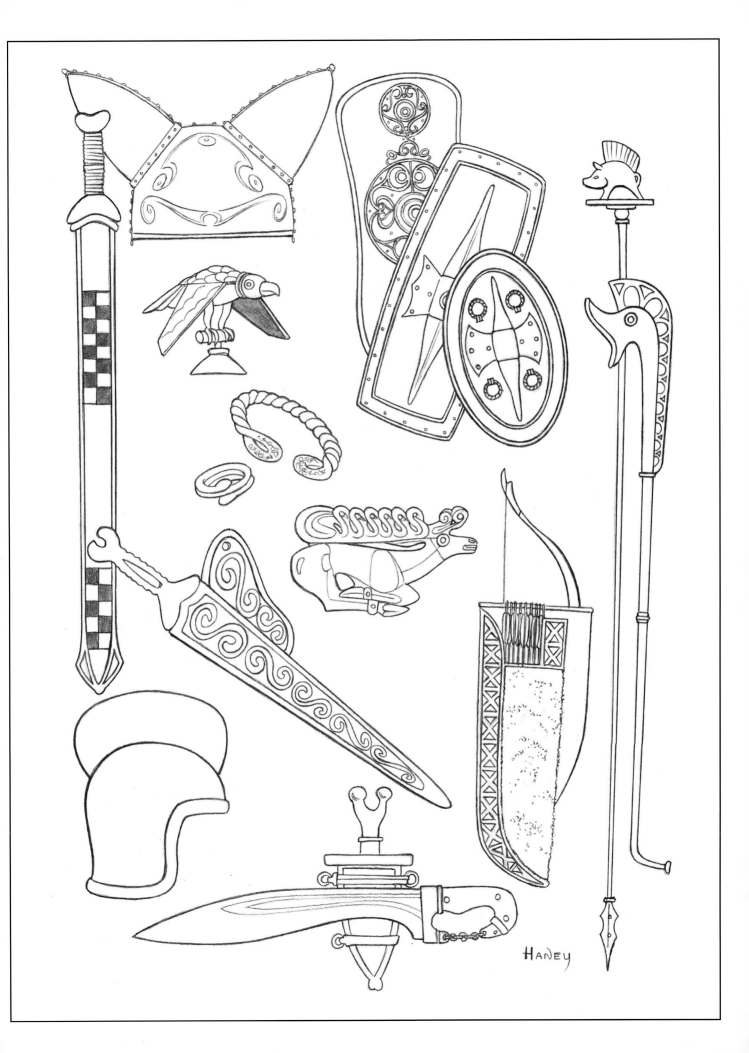

HANEY

Barbarian Arms and Armour

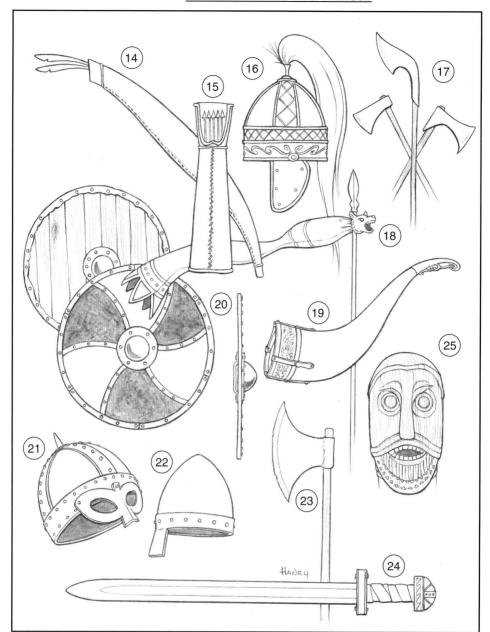

Silver Viking amulet in the form of the hammer belonging to Thor, the Nordic god of thunder, 10th century.

Towards the end of the Roman Empire, Germanic influences began to predominate in Europe. Roman soldiers copied many attributes of Germanic warfare and drawing 16 shows a Goth helmet of the 4th century of the type known as the spangenhelm, a helmet of metal segments secured by rivets to a browband, which became the model for many late Roman helmets; further protection is provided by cheek guards. The Frankish throwing axe, or franciska, shown here in drawing 17 in various forms from the 5th century, was one of the few barbarian weapons not taken up by the Roman army.

Despite the dominance of the German tribes throughout the Roman Empire, during its collapse and in the kingdoms formed afterwards, steppe tribes continued to exert an influence on the fringes. Attila's Huns were later recruited as mercenaries by the Byzantines, long after their notorious leader was dead, in campaigns against the Vandals in North Africa. Drawing 14 shows a Hun bowcase containing a composite bow, one of the most powerful bows available in the early medieval world. The Avars succeeded to the dominance of the Huns in central Europe, at one time ravaging the lands of the Carolingians. Drawing 15 is an Avar quiver of the 7th century and drawing 18 depicts an Avar silk and bronze banner of the "wind-sock" variety, 8th century.

The Vikings were really the last wave of Germanic barbarians to assault the settled civilisations of Romano-Christian Europe. Their helmets were derived from earlier Germanic models, but with variations of their own. Drawing 21 is based on the Gjermundbu helmet with its "spectacle" eye-guards, from Norway, 10th century. The simpler conical helmet with nasal guard in drawing 22 became popular from the 9th to 12th centuries and is most readily associated with the Normans, descendants of the Vikings in northern France. Other typical Vikings objects are the 8th century drinking horn with iron fittings, drawing 19, circular Viking shields with iron bosses, drawing 20, the broad-bladed Viking battle-axe, drawing 23, and a Viking sword, 9th to 10th centuries, drawing 24. Drawing 25 shows a wooden wagon ornament of the 9th century from Norway, perhaps showing the face of a Viking warrior with beard.

HANEY